THE Human Side OF Profitability

BUILDING A BETTER BUSINESS THROUGH PEOPLE

NICOLE MARTIN
CEO, HRBoost, LLC.

Published by:
Nicole Martin
CHICAGO, IL

www.nicolemartin.live

ISBN: 978-0-692-99614-0

Printed in the United States of America

Contents

The Human Side of Profitability

An Introduction

My entire life's work led me to a pivotal place in time when a respected attorney I know asked me to write about human resources. Not the legislative environment or the most recent regulation. Honestly, the external influences on the field are ever-changing however; to think of the true nature of the field I found my fundamental beliefs. These have arisen from working through my own career evolution while being true to myself. Evolving to the point of realizing that once I was keenly aware of my very own drivers, values and burning desires it was clear that my work was in fact my play. Not an effortless journey, but a meaningful one, and not without determination or a demonstration in faith.

Once I realized that I could apply my innate strengths to work, my work, in fact, became play. It is evident that every CEO I have ever worked for is, in essence, doing exactly that. The clarity of this realization has provided an undeniable calling to overcome fear and become willing to work in service. Not for my own pleasure, I now realize, but for something greater. I have found great reward in pursuing my own passions and realizing the things I take for granted are in fact helpful to others. Thus, my fundamental beliefs were born. In this book, I would like to share them with you as a basis for you to build a better business through your people.

Nicole Martin, 2017

Fundamental Belief #1

Every person deserves to find work that plays on his or her strengths.

Every person deserves to do what they excel at naturally. If we all did that, perhaps the diversity of strengths in each of us could develop excellence in our work. This is not a new discovery and many have written about it before. Yet, day in and day out, I fail to observe people readily living their strengths, let alone, leaders that are leading their teams to their strengths. Often, I wonder if people are truly asking themselves, "If I did not have to work but only had to wake up each day and play, what would I do at play?" To be granted the freedom to be free to do exactly this is seen as a dream. Something unattainable, yet I believe it is attainable. With their answer they would find their true calling. Very few in fact do this. From my experience, I see firsthand that the founder of every business I encounter is certainly excelling at what they enjoy and are likely doing so with what comes to them naturally. It would seem obvious that those that come to work for others need only know this truth to be joyful and excellent in their own right. If every employee knew their own drivers, strengths, and values were in alignment with the position, the revenue drivers and values of the business, would it not be clear they would enjoy the work they perform?

I had dinner with a friend recently and she openly declared, "I do not need to like my work, I just need to go!" I completely disagree. I believe that if every leader looked to the workforce with the intent to vet the talent with this form of alignment in mind, the work would in fact be gratifying. The critical factor is to have a relationship to be able to engage the talent in a discussion of authenticity and mutual respect. Personal gratification in work aligned to strengths is not only feel good advice but grounded in behavioral psychology as well as industrial/organizational psychology. It works and translates to the bottom line.

We have traditionally understood job performance through a two-part model: attitude, values, and motivation beside experience, skills and education. Experts and historical reference tell us that when employers are faced with performance problems they typically look to the employee. If experience and skills were present, then it used to be viewed that motivation must be the problem. Much has been researched and done with respect to studies in motivation. One of the outcomes has been to use incentives. Employers would aim to motivate employees with incentives or threaten consequences for non-performance. Circumstances vary but predominately, the studies over the years have demonstrated that this approach would fail to motivate. If employees were motivated and performance was not satisfactory, it is common for management to presume the need for training or more experiential learning.

Clearly, everyone can find themselves in a learning curve. Sometimes the training works and employers realize the benefits as well as the return on investment. Sometimes the experience on the job is developed and the learning curve ends. Many times, however, the curve does not end and the training just does not appear to make a difference.

When making a hiring decision, would it make sense to start with the CAN DO information? The "CAN DO" is what you cannot change with coaching or training after hiring someone. Once you have confirmed which candidates CAN DO the job, behavioral interviewing can help you make the best selection from the favorable candidates. For years, employers of choice have used tools available on the market to assess talent. May I add, not necessarily the best talent but rather the best talent for their business? With validated and reliability tested tools, an employer can see what could be changed and what would not change with training and coaching. Behavioral Assessments can give employers and their respective candidates the information they need for true talent acquisition and development. Even better, leaders can hire strategically and engineer a team for diversity and strength. The cognitive abilities and personality traits describe what the candidate CAN DO.

The most beneficial tools I have used in practice are validated to cognitive ability, normative scores, solid psychometrics, and hard-wired personality traits. Furthermore, they are integrated with critical performance factors and are intended for business use. I have found in working with people throughout my career, many people are not self-aware of their innate strengths or how best to apply them in their work, let alone within the framework of the team they work within. Leaders in business can utilize assessment tools to enhance their recruitment process for improved outcomes. In addition, high performers can be assessed for critical factors in management for educational development and succession. The best of them are well intended not only for the business but for the talent as well, thus providing the information to allow a person to appreciate the factors for which they naturally excel.

This has become something I have incorporated into my own business as it grows. I did not just happen upon it. In fact, I have experienced many tools in my career in human resources but had always thought, "Those are nice but I know how to assess talent; I have reviewed thousands of resumes!" Not necessarily. I, too, am guilty of interview bias. I had interviewed and hired a member to my own team shortly after experiencing growth. Thrilled and confident this person would be a great fit, I extended the offer prematurely. She had the skills and experience it seemed and she was joyful, extroverted, and approachable. Within a week, it was clear it was not working for her or the team. This was a unique opportunity for me to experience what I witness first hand in serving others in management. Had I used then the tools I recommend now, I would have found she did not have the degree of assertiveness that a consultative role requires. Not every HR role is the same in fact. As my team grows, I have found the benefit of truly practicing what we preach and identifying not what I perceive everyone's strengths are but what they truly are. The team is affirmed in their strengths and we bring transparency to them so all can appreciate the diversity of strength for the benefit of the team.

The tools I speak of are not for the mere purpose of improving communication. Those tools are on the market as well but do less to help an individual past the assessment and on their way to success in work dynamics. As you build your team, as you grow your business, do not just hire for the position but with the team and business in mind as well. By understanding this first, it can be easily communicated and allow you to intentionally create a solid foundation by way of communicating your own innate talents as a leader and seeing that any candidate fits the needs of the team with talents that complement and add to its capabilities. In team engineering workshops I have worked with, established teams may appear diverse at first glance but when you review the team behavioral profile, the diversity may exist in areas that lead to contention when working together. Diversity initiatives excel when they are designed to bring people together vs. to highlight differences. It seems simple and, with the right philosophy, it is.

Why is this fundamental belief # 1? Because it will become advantageous when the skilled workforce is not readily available and your talent pool lacks experience.

Fundamental Belief #2

The Talent Deficit is here and talent gets to choose where it wants to work.

The talent pool provides for some alarming statistics in coming years. It is no surprise that 70% of Generation X (1965–1980) desire to be entrepreneurs themselves. In 2015 and beyond, the demographic shifts are leading to a framework where talent will have the luxury to choose where they work. The term office is now a verb for the talent of the future. Let us take a moment to define talent. There is the textbook definition of natural aptitude or skill and then the more typical talent acquisition view of experienced, meaning having knowledge or skill in a particular job or activity. To source seasoned talent indicates a great deal of experience in a particular activity and will require going beyond traditional tactical recruitment methods. In fact, some verticals of business have begun to find little seasoned talent readily available. There is evidence that the Fortune 500 companies have been making talent development a priority for years. Learning and Development Officers oversee full sponsorship training programs for successful talent succession for the business to meet demand in coming years. The make or buy equation in talent sourcing clearly points to the value of a strong talent development strategy linked closely to business strategy and thus outcomes.

On average, 10,000 Baby Boomers (1946-1964) retire every day. There are roughly 45 million individuals that identify as Generation X (1965-1980). Forbes® has published that by the year 2025, Generation Y (1980-2000) will represent 75% of the global workforce. The simple math tells us that we are about to enter a talent gap of approximately 30 million people between now and when larger segments of the millennial generation enter the workforce. Furthermore, as young talent enters into the workforce, there will be a deficit of experienced leaders. This solidifies two critical concerns for every leader at the helm of a business enterprise. One, for the vision to be strategized, implemented and lived, it will require people. People are not a commodity thus this is a variable that poses some complexity. Talent attraction, development and retention factors will be driving factors for every business seeking to grow throughout the next twenty years. This is a concept that every leader must comprehend. In an age where the job market swings cyclically toward and away from career seekers advantage, much of the responsibility for attracting top talent rests with leadership.

If you are the leader of your business, you must become the one that must inspire others to a cause or purpose that brings diverse people together. The entrepreneurial spirit and passion can be contagious. With experienced Generation X rising to the occasion, and Generation Y taking stride through technology and the search for meaningful work, it will be no surprise when many new businesses take shape and flourish. The continued acceleration of change continues to place greater emphasis on the role of Human Resources (HR) practices to develop effective strategies for the current and future workforce. For us to truly be strategic, everything we design, implement, and measure should forecast into the future for sustainability. Not only do you need to identify revenue driving competencies, but also, what does the organization need two, three, five years into the future, considering a segment of your talent will leave voluntarily and you may need to source more? What gaps will exist? Will training alone address the gap and what lead times will exist for a return on the investment? Will it be enough?

Year after year, I work with CEO after CEO and I witness the complexities that develop when these simple truths are not identified and upheld—transparent to all, reinforced consistently, and communicated time and time again. Communication in words and in action is credibility. Credibility in business is currency in business and I often ask leaders I work with, "How credible are you?" Leaders must consistently identify customer values but also internal core values—revenue drivers as they relate to skill competency, strength, and strategy. The leader must be cognizant of these issues for the sake of people and the business. As you expand your business, you must constantly consider what talent looks like for you.

Fundamental Belief #3

The HR-to-Employee ratio does not work (And it is not a 1-800 number).

It is a misconception that an organization does not need dedicated HR support upon inception of the business enterprise. In fact, I believe that even one employee equally presents opportunity as a potential brand ambassador for the business. In contrast, every employee can also be a potential liability. Allow me to explain: early in my career, I was taught that the HR-to-Employee ratio was 1 to 100. Of course, this metric is long outdated. Yet, it seems I continue to discover businesses that operate under this premise.

"Why do I need HR, and what do I need exactly?"... This is a question I rarely get and yet I believe it is the first question that should be asked. In fact, the question I more often hear after explaining what I provide is, "What is HR? Because what you just explained is not what I thought of when I think of HR." Another favorite is, "How does HR impact business profitability?" The simple answer is "significantly." If you have one employee, you have at least 35 laws that apply to your business, many of which require you to do something and be proactive, however, these myriad workplace challenges are often unclear to the untrained eye.

About a month ago, I was on a call with a successful CEO. As we talked freely, he shared that he enjoyed our conversation, but that HR did not "impact his organization." *(This was only moments after he explained he had some legal troubles with former personnel to the tune of "settlements.")* He has chosen to outsource his HR services to a Professional Employer Organization, commonly referred to as a "PEO provider," which I believe is valid given his organizational size; however, his choice in outsourcing seems not to have prevented him from taking hits to his bottom line.

There are several variations on the PEO models that exist today, differing in the nature of the relationship formed between PEO and Client Company. PEO models are typically co-employer relationships. In 2012, according to the National Association of Professional Employer Organizations (NAPEO), there now are approximately 700 PEOs operating in all fifty states. Three such firms caught some negative publicity recently when three PEO owners and one former employee were sentenced in a $133M fraud scheme; the case was high profile and investigated by agents with the Federal Bureau of Investigation and the Internal Revenue Service-Criminal Investigation Division. Overall, the PEO market was responsible for approximately $81B in gross revenue in

2010. Thus, outsourcing HR is big business. Other HR service organizations include Administrative Services Organizations (ASO). These models provide the principal difference between the two types being of service (PEO vs. ASO). In contrast, in an ASO arrangement, the employer remains the employer of record for tax purposes, thus the limitation of the employer's liability is merely perception *(if it is perceived at all).*

There is certainly a space for such service providers but I must share that in my experience, I have learned two things key to the employee and employer relationship. Discretionary loyalty and effort is not tapped over the phone and I believe I would be hindered, despite my experience, to serve a leader well without being onsite, reviewing the files, meeting the people, and learning the business. With that being said, throughout my years in the field, I have worked in organizations as large as a Fortune 500 with 6000+ employees situated internationally to as few as 10 employees in my consultant practice. In my experience, if I waited for the CEOs I worked for to call me, it would often be too late and I would be working towards cost containment vs. cost avoidance or prevention. However, I firmly believe the relevance of outsourcing can be compelling. Considerations must be given to enabling the presence of HR practices in an organization for the benefit of the business not solely for compliance. The objective should not be to simply eliminate transactional responsibilities but rather automate what is necessary and providing little value adds.

One must still align what is necessary, thus tactical components should not be designed in a silo. There are hundreds of tactical components that must align to uphold strategic HR tactics, as both relate to the profitability of the business. For example, a company can put an incentive or recognition program in place. Such a program could easily be established and in fact automated, readily available to managers and/or employees. To do this alone is not enough. Leaders must identify success through reward in such a way that it reinforces the value system, the desired behaviors, and the revenue driving competencies that define success. Often, the tactical components of HR are set forth with a lack of connection to the strategic tactics.

Fundamental Belief #4

Business must have tactical (transactional) and (strategic) HR plans aligned to fully optimize and witness (transformational) work.

I have witnessed the outsourcing phenomenon that has taken place in recent years. In fact, I often see marketing campaigns for HR "optimization" with respect to outsourcing. In my opinion, optimization has more to do with how a business structures its personnel on an organizational level and the methods used to organize how work flows through the business to align with the business' objectives to carry out the business strategy, not just the tactical necessities. How can a business experience "optimization" to the point of transformational HR, if the business seeks only to "optimize" the tactical necessities meanwhile neglecting the strategic HR tactics that will truly "optimize" the business strategy? I believe in the relevance of outsourcing, especially for organizations that find it cost prohibitive to employ a full service HR department. Regardless, I suggest careful consideration of the presence of strategic interplay between business strategy and HR strategy integration to realize the benefits of how HR can "optimize" the business not just the tactical components.

It was 2007 when I, as the Director of HR for a mid-size printed circuit board manufacturer, was presented the PEO services of a large provider targeting small and mid-size businesses. I recall finding how fantastic the tactical streamlining could be, as it would allow a strategic minded HR professional to focus primarily on strategic business initiatives that are often put on the back burner for the sake of day-to-day tactical necessities. However, smaller businesses are being sold on the fact that these models are full service HR. Yet, they can lack the strategy of HR in alignment with the business strategy, if in fact they stand alone. In my case, it was cost prohibitive for the business I served to accept the proposal for the services presented, even if the business had elected to replace my position entirely. I have come to the conclusion that, while there are software platforms on the market that can streamline much that is transactional in HR, those systems alone cannot help a business to realize the truly strategic benefits true HR "optimization" can deliver.

The challenge for the smaller business is that often a growing enterprise can lack the time and resources to build infrastructure and processes that are beyond core business objectives. Typically, beyond attracting talent, entrepreneurs can miss the fact that HR process can be core and ultimately foundational in order for the smaller business to have the same competitive advantage through its people that larger organizations create with size. To do this, every tactic in HR can be designed to specifically reinforce business strategy. The off the shelf, tactical approach that represents the mechanics of HR delivery vs. fully integrated HR Strategy can truly be a competitive disadvantage. This is especially true if the policy, program, process, and even template form documents, etc. are not designed with the strategy of the business itself in mind. Both small and large businesses must attract talent, develop, and retain the best talent for their business. Both must comply with ever changing state and federal regulations and global competition. Both must be concerned with issues related to compensation, benefits, training, employee grievance resolution, and cost control.

Every business must operate between the constructs of efficiency and effectiveness. Efficiency is short-term thinking and effectiveness is long-term thinking. Analysis must be allotted by HR perspectives working with leadership to define how organizational theory interprets the current business strategy and the internal and external environment with respect to contextual and structural dimensions. The actual strategy and structure of a business cannot be optimized, if HR strategy is not related in this context.

There are literally hundreds of tactical HR functions that support eleven HR tactics throughout the employee lifecycle. These eleven tactics are: ***Talent Acquisition,***

Talent Attraction, Compensation, Benefits, Payroll/Tax Administration, Performance Management, Workplace Liability Management, Workplace Safety Management/ Worker's Compensation, Employment Compliance, Recordkeeping/HRIS Technology, *and* ***Separation***.

These eleven HR tactics support seven strategic areas that can drain, restrain, and threaten profitability when not managed properly. The seven strategic areas include: ***HR Expense Management (short term), Leveraging HR Time (HR Administration), Business and Asset Protection, Long Term HR Cost Containment (Health, WC, SUI), Turnover Reduction, Talent Attraction and Employee Productivity.***

Each of the aforementioned HR tactics and strategies has the ability to maximize profitability through Human Resources by influencing the bottom line. At the same time that small HR improvements can dramatically increase profits, it is just as simple for small HR mistakes to devastate the bottom line. Small mistakes are missed when the trained eye is not in your process, observing your practice and in line with your vision.

While I agree that HR can be an overhead department, I would argue that not every HR solution has to be and, in all actuality, I have seen more profit lost to CEOs knowing full well each circumstance could have been prevented had a trained eye been involved in the process. In fact, the first time a CFO told me HR was overhead and had little value, I began working to prove him wrong and, within twelve months on the team, our organization had been recognized as one of Best and Brightest Companies to Work For™. Back in 2005, I was pleasantly surprised; I was just seeking access to benchmark quantitative data. Examining engagement metric tracking by company size, the SHRM GloboForce 2012 Winter Survey results showed us that larger companies are more likely to measure employee engagement than smaller ones (65% vs. 30%). Needless to say, I have befriended every CFO I have encountered since, as the collaboration of HR and Finance in driving quantitative and qualitative data is something every business should be doing. The difference then was that I was a peer to Finance and having the support of leadership was pivotal to my ability to be effective in the HR leadership role.

It has been well known for years that there is a link between workforce engagement and corporate performance. In fact, the term "engagement" is the entire buzz. The term itself fails to truly capture what I have experienced in a culture as such because I believe the word "engagement" can seem too tentative. I have become fonder of the term "entanglement" so coined in the book, "It's my Company, Too!" by Kenneth R. Thompson, Thomas J. Walter, Ramon L. Benedetto and Molly Meyer.

Companies that achieve qualitative and quantitative yield on engagement have achieved something more. Of 75 possible drivers of engagement, the one that was rated as the most important was the extent to which employees believed that their senior management had a sincere interest in their well-being. In fact, Towers Watson has published studies reporting that companies with high engagement enjoy 3x the operating margin. Other key factors to increases in revenue are attributed to 95% of employees believing they had the work tools and resources they needed to perform exceptionally, compared to only 20% in contrasting organizations. Similar disparities appeared with regard to the ability to sustain energy throughout the workday (97% vs. 32%) and a sense of personal accomplishment at work (99% vs. 33%). However, only 38% of the Canadian respondents believed their organization and senior leaders encouraged and supported a healthy workforce and just 39% thought senior leaders were sincerely interested in their wellbeing. In 2012, PwC reported that engagement and involvement are critical in managing change at work yet nine out of ten of the key barriers to the success of change programs are people-related. There you have it! Business goes nowhere fast without people.

A Best & Brightest winner would rather re-post a job than give the position to a candidate who is not a fit. The culture of a company such as this is protected. The impact of a poor placement is viewed as more expensive than the delay in placement. I often observe many leaders in business discuss and debate the nature of culture. I believe every business has an opportunity to express an invitation to a culture. It is the invitation, in fact, that requires careful consideration and development. When done well, talent is able to self-identify, if the values of the business align with personal values. It is the invitation that establishes the intended culture but it is every communication, decision, and behavior that follows in practice that, in fact, becomes the culture. Whether the lived culture and the invitation to culture are expressed as one is the basis for shared vision. As an entrepreneur and leader of a business, the vision is yours to establish and communicate for a shared vision.

For HR strategy to integrate to optimize business strategy, the HR professional must understand external influences on your business as well as the internal value proposition that clearly communicates what is in it for employees. Why? What is the fundamental purpose of it all? To drill to that level of meaning is essential. HR must know business objectives in order to integrate HR initiatives that strategically support the workforce in performing to meet those objectives. I once referred to myself as conduit and a gentlemen, a highly respected veteran of our military and leader in his own right, corrected me and declared that I was a weaver. Honestly, HR should be able to tie your business strategy directly to their HR strategy, which in turn supports management and provides visibility and transparency to employees with respect to their role in achieving it. It must be reinforced and reinstated time and again. Everyone must feel part of "it," whatever "it" is!

Fundamental Belief #5

Every manager of the future needs to be a manager of choice.

With new leadership development programs or current management onboarding initiatives, there will need to be more discussed than functional skill. The *State of the American Workplace: Employee Engagement Insights for U.S. Business Leaders* report highlights findings from Gallup's ongoing study of the American workplace from 2010 through 2012. Findings clearly demonstrate that, in the most recent year, 70% of Americans do not love their boss. Thus, knowing what managers of choice look like from the beginning is important when considering employees as brand advocates for your business. Not to mention, the investments leaders make in the talent in hopes of realizing the return on investment.

Managers of choice are good at talent scouting to build their teams, relationship building, trust building, skill building, and organization brand building. How many leadership development programs do you come across with those top five competencies? Once the foundational purpose for a business is identified and the business experiences growth, it is important to acquire talent as well as acquire and/or develop managers of choice. If you are striving to be credible as the leader of your business, it is a must to practice being a leader of choice on the journey to your own vision to support the team. Given talent development is a critical factor for a thriving business, it is important to define not just the best talent out there but the best talent for you, your business, and your team.

Fundamental Belief #6

Every person must have a clear explanation of what success looks like in each respective role and for the business overall.

Communication is critical to the role of every leader in the business and the challenge as your business grows will be to maintain the access and/or visibility of the shared vision for the employees across the business. Maintaining a shared vision will require leaders to communicate it clearly and often enough that employees feel part of it. The words alone will not be enough as communicating the shared vision is as essential as living it out in actions.

Relationship management skills become increasingly important in order for a manager to provide feedback communicated with care and respect. Ideally, real feedback in real time, when possible, and peer accountability is a wonderful component to a framework for accountability. This is built into communication forums and technology tools today but the face-to-face exchange strengthens it. Many can find their performance management process stuck in neutral and many employees feel their managers are unskilled at discussing performance let alone coaching to performance. Despite those two factors, not a single one of us can ignore that it is an important process that has the potential to motivate an employee to organizational objectives and keep them inspired on their own journey to excellence. Performance is only one factor to consider given the fact that talent development will be critical to the majority of businesses.

Developmental potential and learning and development plans will begin to allow for strategic talent pipelines. A design initiative such as this is a collaborative process between functional experts and should build on revenue driving competency development. Ultimately, the make or buy equation with talent is unique to the talent pool, the turnover ratio, and the lead time required to establish competency. The emergency evolves as you hone in on your demand. Every employee should be able to identify how to plug themselves into the business. When done well, it should build on what they excel in naturally and the definition of success should be reinforced each day, each week, each month, each quarter, and annually whenever possible. The identification of success should be readily available, simple to assimilate and ideally, objective. And, if personal values are to align with business values, the framework for behaviors must also be developed and upheld. Without a clear definition of success, the objective can become vague and the culture will suffer.

I have a client that is a serial entrepreneur. I have found him to be extremely effective in his work. He has metrics for all transactions for his team and every employee tied to a revenue-driving competency has a metric goal. Years into the business, we met and he was observing that the employees did not understand that the metric goal was in fact the expectation. This is a function of performance management. Expectations are not goals and thus should never be communicated as such. We were able to redesign his job descriptions to include indicators of effectiveness for not only competencies but also specific measurements. In addition, the metrics as well as the effectiveness definitions allowed for transparency on what is necessary to reach the next level of performance.

An effective leader absolutely must establish the definition of success. The challenge presents itself when the roles are not revenue driving but rather support departments. This is common in sales organizations with administrative infrastructure. Correlating the effectiveness of those departments as they relate is an opportunity in inclusion and team performance. And, when it is overlooked, the crux of a functional structure takes hold and silos emerge.

Think about these two sentiments commonly rated in engagement surveys: "The purpose of my company makes me feel my job is important." and "I am clear on my organizations goals and future direction and the way in which I contribute to them." Last but not least, help employees know how to express what they would hope to gain in experiences by communicating career advocacy. Aim to retain what you invest in and remember to identify not the best people, but the best people given their role, the team, and the business need. If someone is failing, every leader should ask him or herself why. This is a critical exercise in self-evaluation as a manager of choice before moving immediately to a call for separation. True, circumstances can prevail, but this question should always be part of the process.

Fundamental Belief #7

As the CEO, the Founder, and/or the Entrepreneur, you must lead!

Do not ever underestimate your role as a leader. Embrace the power and responsibility to create an environment where people love to come to work.

The best workplace cultures exist in companies that value two-way communication. Employees are often *expected* to make decisions to improve the company vs. the traditional hierarchical decision making model. Companies that value communication use Intranet and Social Media tools to communicate with employees. They still have town hall meetings, pep talks, and team huddles. Collecting qualitative data is as important as quantitative data, when it comes to the workforce. They were not the companies that blocked Facebook or LinkedIn from their websites, but rather the ones that took the lead in educating their employees how to represent the business as a brand ambassador on their profiles. They use webcasts and one in four has blogs from senior leaders. In culture assessments, employees can be asked whether or not they agree with the following statement: "When good or bad things happen at my organization, employees hear about it in a timely manner." The CEOs I have served understand that very few things are truly confidential and often the absence of communication can lead to far worse assumptions than the actual truth.

I was talking with an employee at one of my client's locations. The employee cited information shared with her from another leader which should have been communicated to her directly, but was not. The CEO in this instance lost credibility. I cannot express how damaging the most innocent of communications, or lack thereof, can mitigate the ability to tap into the employee's commitment level. Something as simple as common courtesy and discretion is still valued and what good news, right? What is often missed is that this is also a symptom of a CEO that decided to manage in a moment where they should have led. Employees take offense, if they hear about something significant from the grapevine vs. management.

I often witness leaders that own a business having a hard time leading after they hire talent to manage. Honestly, the philosophy behind communication should not be fear in communicating there is a pay freeze. Rather, a leader should confidently, bring the team together to inspire the change needed to impact a positive outcome. I have witnessed businesses thrive after significant challenges including pay freezes, furlough, even disaster recovery. I find myself in awe of the fact that one person may feel they need to solve all the problems of the business. The best leaders ask questions and truly allow other leaders to rise to the occasion.

I have served among great managers and employees that were leaders in their own right. I have witnessed entire manufacturing teams who have worked through Memorial Day weekend simply because they knew their "boss" needed them to. Was there an incentive, you ask? No! I recall this leader going around the back of the CEO, rather than speaking to him about the way in which he would work to the objective. Why? To simply avoid the discussion, and yet all I could see was nearly 100 people that would tie their loyalty to the leader that saw them as adults, real people contributing to the bottom line. They in turn, contributed, felt satisfaction in the collaboration, and never asked once what was in it for them. Yes, I have witnessed discretionary effort and, when it is present, you can feel it in the room. Underneath it all, some observe people at work and I observe people at play. Those people were doing the work for themselves. Examples like the one I share are real. The balance is the leader must not take for granted what has been benefited and gratitude must be expressed and be sincere.

The way that everyone can play is when they sense the passion from the leader, the call to action, if you will. The "why" will bring people that align forth and if each role can be expressed in a way that supports the why sentiment, each person can sense their contribution and can tie their work back to profitability. When asked, I advise to tell the truth and, if it must be withheld, simply share that you are not at liberty to share but appreciate their inquiry. Never outright lie to an employee, lest you lose credibility and trust. Very little is confidential in the end. Being up front is essential for business success; it lets the employee know they matter and, even more important, shows that you care.

Fundamental Belief #8

Every Chief Visionary deserves a Chief Challenger . . . or Challengers!

A key observation in my career working with leadership is that great leaders demonstrate trust by trusting managers to manage up. One example that comes to mind is the CEO that aims to be the unbiased party on the team. You know, Switzerland? At the end of the day, the CEO must understand they will never be viewed as the neutral party by everyone and even more evident is the fact that the CEO plays the role of Chief. That does not mean dictator or even final decision maker; Chief Visionary works, however. Regardless, every Chief deserves an adversary but ideally one that means well and is in fact capable of proactively expressing the contrary perspective.

In my experience I have found it important to advise leaders to have a person on their team that is in fact honest, unafraid, yet caring enough to speak, interrogate the presented view respectfully, and perhaps privately when appropriate. For if you are a leader who always hears affirmations or if there is no drama in your business, then you should be concerned.

Every good team deserves someone that veers from consensus. From my perspective, the Chief Visionary should set the tone and the expectations; this, in fact, is the expressed invitation that inspires. Without commitment to uphold the affinity of the expressed invitation, personality dynamics play out and, before long, someone else's invitation will have been accepted. Often, when I meet with individual managers that comprise a team, it is shocking how many crave the invitation and yet, without the presence of a trusted neutral presence, many opt out of the conversation.

The importance of good collaborative exchange is to remember that constructive brainstorming sessions and dialogue between leaders must occur for the sake of the business. Furthermore, it is important to not concede in agreement for peace but rather listen and strive to understand the nature of disagreement. The Chief Visionary's role is to uphold the vision and values of the business, never sacrificing respect for the contributors. This requires the Chief Visionary to set the tone.

This belief I share with the sole intention of arming you with secrets to some of the best I have had the pleasure of working for. Seek the debate and provide for the neutral exchange free of perceived retribution. Never forget: perception is reality.

Fundamental Belief #9

Accountability counts!

You must walk the talk. In fact, take the open-ended question to the workforce and ask everyone to submit what they define as accountability in their role. It can be an enlightening exercise.

Often the team knows well what a banned behavior is, but is it communicated by the grapevine or by well-established standards? Best case, it is communicated by who gets paid and who gets promoted and, in situations where accountability really matters, it can be seen in who is no longer with the team. Remember, there is not much that remains truly confidential so my best advice is to always lead and manage like everyone knows exactly what took place.

One of the greatest challenges I see good people struggle with is doing good things for others and then getting burned. The old saying, "no good deed goes unpunished," rings true. Something as simple as loaning employees money or allowing something like extended time off for illness or family matters—seemingly simple gestures of kindness–may establish precedent in subsequent similar circumstances in the future. The business may grow, evolve, and hit legal thresholds for protected rights for employees. Thus, it is not a bad practice to ask yourself, "Would I do this with any person working for me now or in the future?"

With my employee relations experience, I can tell you that it should be the Chief Visionary's goal to allow for internal resolution whenever possible. However, keeping all complaints internal vs. external for proper resolution does not mean the fact finding process should be performed by an internal employee, unless that person is trained in such matters. This is imperative to mitigate risk. It is reasonable to presume that people may not feel comfortable approaching the primary leader despite fair intentions. For this reason, it seems prudent to provide another layer that is neutral and unbiased. Any first line managers would require extensive training on various topics to best support an internal complaint procedure without the guidance of an experienced HR or legal professional. Ultimately, if there is not an internal resource and only an internal complaint procedure, then perhaps a confidential phone line could be provided to employees.

Truly great managers demonstrate respect, by managing up and communicating for the sake of exchange and collaboration vs. the sentiment of reporting up and perceiving micro management. I have seen good managers derail their career by not understanding that unrequested status reports are not micro managing. Rather, it is the gift of peace of mind that every manager can give their leader.

Last, but certainly not least: tell the TRUTH. People talk about how accountability is broken and how people avoid difficult conversations; why? Some say it is a lack of standards, consistency, or follow-through. That may be true, but at the true core of the breakdown is communication. Everyone deserves to hear the truth. In fact, I believe it is the responsibility of leadership to deliver the truth. And on occasion it will be equally important to ask for the truth.

Leadership must uphold the integrity to work through the communication breakdowns to provide for unity and shared vision. If necessary, begin with the belief that everyone comes to work with the hope to do well. Yes, there are some that do not operate within that statement in reality, but if you can begin with the glass half full, it may allow the communication needed to be set forth. You can explain to anyone the truth so long it is done with respect and sensitivity. Respect means it does not get personal and sensitivity implies the need to ask questions not diagnose. Ask and you may find something you were not aware of.

If you are the person that finds it difficult to communicate proactively or address difficult situations without compromising fact with emotions, then I recommend a simple four step process to facing the conversation head on with dignity and respect in mind. I hope it is easy to remember and works in bridging your communications with direct reports.

Step One: Begin with "I expect (insert)…."

Step Two: Contrast and highlight the concern by stating next, "I observe (insert)…."

Step Three: Lastly, do not diagnose or speculate as to the cause; avoid judgment as a first course and ask, "Why is that?"

Step Four: End by reaffirming the expectation. Clarify misunderstanding and recalibrate.

This conversation is important in the most basic of circumstances. Not to speak or to avoid is to express acceptance (and, in some cases, agreement). Those that gauge credibility and trust daily take note.

Fundamental Belief #10

Welcome, welcome, welcome the talent!

Orientation is more than paperwork and onboarding can be more than a day, a week, or a month. Your Employee Value Proposition (EVP) is as important, if not more so, as your Unique Selling Proposition (USP). Your brand is not what you *say* you are, but rather what your customers *experience* and what your employees *believe.*

From passive recruitment to talent pipeline and even your alumni, the campaign for "Welcome, Welcome, and Welcome!" should be heard. A customized onboarding strategy for all new hires across the organization, from the day they accept the position to potentially their variable career paths within the organization, is ideal. The onboarding term can itself imply enculturation.

To design a framework strategically, the business should strive to support the employees' ability to perform and contribute. This would include expectations, clear lines to what success is at intervals tied to formal coaching and/or feedback exchange with management, access to peers or mentors with knowledge on internal networks, and I believe it should be implemented in a phased approach. (Often information can be too much, if it is not phased with consideration to how and when the talent can best assimilate it for practical purposes.)

It is surprising how many businesses fail to connect strategic objectives to every person on the team. There is nothing more offensive than to witness *The Mushroom Theory of Management*. When a human being is giving energy, strength, and time to his or her work, it is easy to understand that every person deserves to be informed of what is relevant. If there is a sentiment that "they will not understand" or "they don't care," then please be the leader that challenges assumptions by stating that "we can teach." Most of what "they will not understand" or "they don't care" about is, in fact, relevant.

Take the time to onboard and teach your staff about your business, clarify expectations, and highlight employee education opportunities. Forget the perceived "soft stuff;" use hard data to determine if results have been met and explain which measures to aim for to achieve success. Remember that transparency is more important than pay. Celebrate team successes and consider profit-based pay programs. If you fail to start with the people that represent your brand, how can you positively affect the customer and build a competitive advantage?

Management assimilation is another opportunity for every business that intends to grow. Forty percent (40%)

of promoted leaders fail in their new role in the first 18 months. The cost is significant and negatively impacts the ability to uphold consistency and credibility. Every person that is hired requires onboarding, even the most seasoned of professionals. There are positive ways to support the assimilation of management and strategically every business will need to focus on this initiative proactively vs. reactively. I have seen truly wonderful managers become ineffective simply because their leader did not lead by clearly establishing expectations, gaining commitment, and establishing a shared vision.

Fundamental Belief #11

Never be cured of your curiosity!

In closing, I would like to share some learning moments that may prove valuable for you. Here are a few memories that really stand out to me:

1. I was working as a receptionist in an international Fortune 500 enterprise and I observed dozens of people in the lobby each day for hours (essentially, people hired under H1-B Visas prior to Y2K). It was a time of panic that preceded the year 2000, as fear was present in the financial services industry. I thought it was a drain on resources and particularly unkind to keep people waiting for hours with no guidance. I created an orientation program for these people and presented it to the site manager, proactively, for approval. I had no clue what Human Resources was but that man saw something in me, at the young age of 18, and explained to me that I belonged in Human Resources. I was promoted into the field and to this day I am forever grateful.

The lesson: *If you are a leader and see youthful talent before you, then teach, share, and nurture that talent. Thank you, Jack Egan, for seeing my strengths long before I knew to recognize them for myself. And to Leigh Harte, my* *first manager in HR, thank you for believing in my potential and allowing me to feel part of the bigger picture every day we worked together. Had you never left, I likely would not have either.*

2. I had to support a large layoff with people I had worked with for years. It was sudden, done with pink slips, and totaled 300 individuals. It was the first time in my life I had seen and felt how business can treat people like numbers vs. people.

The lesson: *There is a right way and a wrong way to deliver bad news. Though I have had to do this type of work since, I will never partake in a termination meeting that is done without care for a person's sense of dignity.*

3. I landed my first HR Manager position in Chicago, Illinois at a privately held ink pump manufacturer. I found myself in the midst of an Office of Federal Contract Compliance Programs (OFFCP) audit in my first six weeks in the role. New to the role, I knew little of the historical hiring practices. The audit involved specific review of the Affirmative Action plan in place and, specifically, the applicant records directly related to positions posted and filled against evaluation of the placed individuals in given roles. The end result led to fines specific to each applicant that met the minimum qualifications on the job posting but had not been evaluated. (Meaning that applicants who applied to the job posting and were seemingly qualified were not interviewed; the questions were "Why not?" and "What disqualified them?") The end result was upwards of $50,000 awarded in settlement.

The lesson: *Surely, it would seem I learned the importance of record keeping, interview training, and standardization in hiring practices. The real lesson was that as well intended as employers may be, and as justified as the hiring decision may have been, the bottom line is that businesses are impacted significantly by external influences and ignorance is not bliss.*

4. I was in the position of hiring for manufacturing positions, along with a peer manager, and we had two interviews scheduled. The first was a no-show who had been eagerly anticipated in review of the resume. The second interview was 30 minutes early and had ridden his bike to the facility. The value in applicant tracking for passive recruitment is that you can monitor who applies repeatedly and how often. After hiring someone with no experience, despite the initial evaluation, we called in a repeat candidate who had applied consistently for two years but had no qualifications. He was willing to start at the bottom—a position no one would take—as he had read about the company in the paper and really wanted the opportunity to get his foot in the door.

The lesson: *Who do you think got the job? Right, the man that found a way to get to the interview on time and the man that applied again and again and again. May character and perseverance always shine in your character assessments and may you evaluate the talent on what they do, not what they say they do.*

5. I was working in HR management and reporting directly to the CEO in another company. There was a longtime manager there who oversaw the production for two or more decades. One day, the CEO called me to explain that it had been reported that the people in production felt I was insincere and overly kind to the point of being "fake!" Needless to say, I was stunned and hurt. I could have easily quit but I did not want to concede to what was not true. I vehemently denied the claims and stated I would see to the people and sit down with their manager. With poise, I confronted the manager and let him know I was there to support the management not control the management and attempting to sabotage HR only hurts management in the end. I further demonstrated how my efforts, though they may feel like more work for him, would help vs. hinder the objectives production had. He apologized, and we never had another negative exchange.

The lesson: *People can be ugly and sadly manipulative but it often stems from misunderstandings and a lack of* *communication. It is a valuable lesson to confront the truth, speak for what you believe in, know the value of HR in support of management, AND the value of loyalty through leadership support. It also taught me the importance of managers not allowing complacency to creep into management exchange due to hurt feelings or disagreements. To have stayed and not confront the manager would have stifled the relationship and the business. The support and affirmation by the CEO of HR as a supporter was a factor to the respect that developed in the years that followed in working with that person. Getting past secondary emotions to build bridges in honoring primary emotions in the workplace is important.*

6. In 2008, I attended the National SHRM Conference and saw the founder, Dr. JP Pawliw-Fry, of the Institute of Health and Human Potential present the Epidemic of Playing Small. In my role, I often witness disagreements, emotions and tempers flare. Not ideal I realize, but something I am quite comfortable in, given my work. Comfortable, however, is different than truly understanding what you are seeing unfold before your eyes. When I sat through this presentation, I found myself move from a lens of judgment to the lens of compassion as I gained a greater understanding of emotional intelligence.

The physiological response that occurs in our brains when we are compromised by stress is an automatic response whereby the hypothalamus releases cortisol – thus elevating blood pressure to help you escape danger. The revealing facts that I had witnessed, but never understood, occurred when I saw two executives come together as tempers flared. One presented facts akin to "I asked for that on Tuesday and it was not delivered," and the other person responded with no recollection or memory. I had been present for the prior exchange between these two and was absolutely perplexed by the lack of recollection of that meeting. Witnessing this next exchange made me think the person must have lost their mind. Well, in fact, they had! Stress affects us all the same physiologically, given the automatic stress response of the release of cortisol. And, in turn, it can inhibit memory retrieval for a period of up to five minutes, as in this example. Shocking but common!

The lesson: *Stress is not universally experienced and thus understanding what triggers stress for different people is the responsibility of each person in understanding behavioral responses that can and do occur at work. Furthermore, Dr. Pawliw-Fry shared his sentiment regarding the importance of teaching that it is okay to say, "I don't know!" In fact, promote it. It is more important to learn, unlearn, adapt, and change vs. to build confidence in the "right answer" or being "smart." I hope to work with many a leader that allows him or her to say, "I don't know" and gain through inclusive brainstorming with diverse mindsets coming together!*

Conclusion

HR may be thought of as an expense and not an asset, but this approach can be disastrous to the bottom line and counterproductive to business objectives. Every person deserves to find work that is in fact their strengths at play. A business with this approach will have a better chance at overcoming the talent deficit. The Talent Deficit is here, and the talent gets to choose where they want to work.

Old norms for running HR departments and formulas for doing so do not work. Companies must be asking why they need HR and what do they need exactly to weave employees into a team that functions to achieve core objectives every day. Business must have tactical (transactional) and (strategic) HR plans aligned to fully optimize and witness (transformational) work, for a business to thrive and lead their industry or market. To do this every manager needs to be a manager of choice and every person in the business must be viewed as a leader and brand ambassador. This also requires that every person in the organization must have a clear explanation of what success looks like in each respective role and for the business overall. To establish core values for a business is not enough. They must be upheld in performance management. This all starts with the CEO who as a CEO, founder, or entrepreneur, must lead. To be effective, every Chief Visionary deserves a Chief Challenger or Challengers. Accountability Counts through every level of the organization and it all starts the first day you hire an employee and welcome talent to your company.

I wish you the best success through your work and in play! May your vision inspire many to bring their talents to a valuable exchange.

Nicole Martin, MSHRM, SPHR, SHRM-SCP
CEO, HRBoost, LLC.

Author, Speaker, Consultant, Futurist

Nicole Martin, a self-professed "country girl in disguise," grew up in Montana. This small town setting, where everyone knows you and greets you on the street, was the foundation for her dedication to transparency and accountability in all ways, both personal and professional. Nicole was fortunate to have a great mentor early in life: her mom. A highly spiritual woman, Nicole's mother raised her with the philosophy of being happy. She ingrained in her the belief that every person is special and unique and that we are each capable of anything.

Following this advice, Nicole didn't hesitate to head out on her own to the big city of Chicago where she received her BS in Business Management & Psychology and her Master's of Science degree in Human Resource Management. While pursuing her degrees, Nicole also worked with a young, Y2K firm struggling to accommodate an influx of programmers arriving from all around the world to ensure their client's computer systems would not be crashing on 1/1/2000. Seeing the chaos, she single handedly created and implemented a training program which resulted in a system to accommodate these new employees and, ultimately, the establishment of their HR department. From that early opportunity and on, Nicole has helped numerous companies build and evolve their businesses into thriving, successful entities. Today Nicole is CEO of her own successful company, dedicated to helping small to mid-size business realize their potential through their employees.

Nicole Martin does her best to share her expertise, not just as a senior executive, but as a futurist, thought leader, public speaker, blogger, internet TV host, author, board member and volunteer. As an ambassador for *101 Best and Brightest Companies to Work For™*, she has helped Chicago and Milwaukee businesses see all the benefits a fully integrated human resources department can bring. "If you go into a business and they are *a 101 Best and Brightest Company to Work For™*, you can feel it. You see on the people's faces, the authenticity, the honesty, constructive criticism *(which is level of respect)* not complacency where managers actually think something in silence and don't communicate it," explains Nicole.

Nicole thrives on helping others by simply following her passion. She helps entrepreneurs understand the importance human resources can play in developing and maintaining a strong, vibrant business. Her expertise provides more to an organization than just a corporate culture boost or a good office vibe. She links **human capital** directly to profitability time and time again—and she's got the analytics path charts and the logic models to prove it.

To learn more about Nicole, her recently released book, ***The Talent Emergency,*** or how you can engage her as a speaker at your next event, please go to *nicolemartin.live* or *talentemergency.com, or email her at info@hrboost.com.*